HOLIDAYS, FESTIVALS, & CELEBRATIONS

VALENTINE'S DAY

BY ANN HEINRICHS · ILLUSTRATED BY SHARON HOLM

Published in the United States of America by The Child's World®
PO Box 326 • Chanhassen, MN 55317-0326
800-599-READ • www.childsworld.com

ACKNOWLEDGMENTS
The Child's World®: Mary Berendes, Publishing Director

Editorial Directions, Inc.: E. Russell Primm, Editorial Director; Katie Marsico, Managing Editor; Judith Shiffer,
Assistant Editor; Caroline Wood and Rory Mabin, Editorial Assistants; Susan Hindman, Copy Editor and
Proofreader; Elizabeth Nellums, Rory Mabin, Ruth Martin, and Caroline Wood, Fact Checkers; Tim Griffin/
IndexServ, Indexer

The Design Lab: Kathleen Petelinsek, Design and Page Production

LIBRARY OF CONGRESS CATALOGING-IN-PUBLICATION DATA
Heinrichs, Ann.
Valentine's Day / by Ann Heinrichs ; illustrated by Sharon Holm.
    p. cm. — (Holidays, festivals, & celebrations)
Includes index.
ISBN 1-59296-583-0 (library bound : alk. paper) 1. Valentine's Day—Juvenile literature. I. Holm, Sharon Lane, ill.
II. Title. III. Series.
GT4925.H45 2006
394.2618—dc22   2005025690

TABLE OF CONTENTS

CHAPTER ONE

HAPPY VALENTINE'S DAY!

Bright red hearts are everywhere. People give each other pretty cards. Gifts of flowers and candy bring warm smiles. It's Valentine's Day!

Valentine's Day is a happy holiday. It celebrates love and friendship.

What's the best greeting for Valentine's Day? Tell someone "I love you." Or just say, "You are special!"

Hearts are a famous symbol for Valentine's Day.

Roses are red,
Violets are blue,
If you'll be my sweetheart,
I'll be yours, too!

CHAPTER TWO

AIMING FOR THE HEART

Many **ancient** peoples had a god of love. For ancient Romans, it was Cupid. Cupid appears as a baby with wings. He carries a bow and arrow. What does he aim for? People's hearts! Whoever is shot falls in love.

Have you seen valentines showing flying babies? They're not angels. They are little Cupids!

Cupid is a knavish lad,
Thus to make poor females mad.
—William Shakespeare
(1564–1616)

Ancient Romans believed Cupid's arrows caused people to fall in love.

A VALENTINE

Go, Cupid, and my sweetheart tell
I love her well.
Yes, though she tramples
    on my heart
And rends that bleeding thing apart;
And though she rolls a scornful eye
On doting me when I go by;
And though she scouts at
    everything
As tribute unto her I bring—
Apple, banana, caramel—
Haste, Cupid, to my love and tell,
In spite of all, I love her well.
—Eugene Field

CHAPTER THREE

CHOOSING SWEETHEARTS

How did Valentine's Day begin? The story goes back more than two thousand years. Ancient Romans held a festival on February 15. It was called Lupercalia (loo-pur-KAY-lee-uh). Spring was coming soon. It was a time to celebrate new life.

Lupercalia was held shortly before the arrival of spring.

'Tis better to have loved and lost,
Than never to have loved at all.
—Alfred Lord Tennyson
(1809–1892)

A special ceremony was held the day before Lupercalia. Girls' names were written on slips of paper. Then they were put into a jar. Each young man drew a girl's name from the jar. The two would be sweethearts during the festival.

In time, the Romans became Christians. They laid aside their old ways. But they would soon have a new holiday for sweethearts.

Ancient Romans drew names from a jar to find out who their sweetheart would be.

CHAPTER FOUR

WHO WAS SAINT VALENTINE?

Valentine's Day is often called Saint Valentine's Day. But who was Saint Valentine? Many **legends** are told about him. One says he was a Christian priest in ancient Rome.

The Roman emperor was building up an army. But married men didn't want to join. They wanted to stay home with their wives. So the emperor outlawed marriage.

There are many legends about Saint Valentine.

Valentine took pity on couples in love. He secretly married them. But his secret was discovered. He was thrown in jail and sentenced to death.

While in jail, he made friends with the jailer's daughter. Before his death, he sent her a good-bye note. He signed it, "From your Valentine."

Valentine was declared a Christian saint. He became the **patron saint** of people in love. It's said that he died on February 14. So that became Saint Valentine's Day.

Saint Valentine wrote a letter to his jailer's daughter.

Life without love is like a tree without blossom and fruit.
—Kahlil Gibran
(1883–1931)

CHAPTER FIVE

A HOLIDAY FOR LOVE

Saint Valentine's Day became a popular holiday. It was a day to celebrate love!

One Valentine's Day custom arose in England and Scotland. Young people put their names in a bowl. Then they drew names to see who their sweetheart would be. They wore the name on their sleeve.

Girls in England had another custom. A girl thought of all the boys she liked. She wrote each one's name on a piece of paper. She rolled each paper up in a ball of clay. Then she put the clay balls in a jar of water. The first name that rose to the top would be her valentine!

Who I am I shall not say,
But I send you this bouquet
With this query, baby mine:
"Will you be my valentine?"
—Eugene Field
*   (1850–1895)*

A number of Valentine's Day games began in England and Scotland.

Oh! if it be to choose
and call thee mine,
Love, thou art every
day my Valentine!
—*Thomas Hood*
(1799–1845)

CHAPTER SIX

Tomorrow is Saint
  Valentine's day,
All in the morning betime,
And I a maid at your
  window,
To be your Valentine.
—William Shakespeare
  (1564–1616)

WHO WILL BE MY VALENTINE?

Many beliefs arose about Saint Valentine's Day. One was that birds chose their mates on February 14. So people believed that they should do the same!

Girls rushed to their windows that morning. They believed the first person they saw would be their valentine. Some girls left nothing to chance. They stood at their sweetheart's window!

A young woman watched for birds that day, too. Was a robin flying overhead? That meant she'd marry a sailor. Did she see a sparrow? Then she would marry a poor man. What if she saw a goldfinch? She would marry a rich man!

Girls used to wait by the window to catch a glimpse of their valentine.

Muse, bid the Morn awake!
Sad Winter now declines,
Each bird doth choose
 a mate;
This day's Saint Valentine's.
—Michael Drayton
(1563–1631)

CHAPTER SEVEN

SYMBOLS OF LOVE

Saint Valentine's Day became a day to write love letters. They were often written as poems. The love notes were called valentines. Young men even proposed marriage in valentines.

By the 1700s, there were valentines for sale. They were beautiful! They were trimmed with lace, silk, and ribbons. Feathers and flowers were attached. Even drops of perfume were added.

These valentines showed many symbols of love. We still see them on valentines today. Bright red hearts are favorites. An arrow often pierces the heart. Who shoots the arrow? Little Cupid, the god of love!

A hundred years would
be too few
To carry all my love for you.
—Author unknown

Pairs of doves are another symbol. They stand for eternal love. Why? Because doves mate for life. Doves also make cooing sounds—like sweethearts do!

Love looks not with the eyes, but with the mind, And therefore is winged Cupid painted blind.
—William Shakespeare (1564–1616)

Doves are a symbol of eternal love.

CHAPTER EIGHT

CELEBRATING LOVE AND FRIENDSHIP

People still like giving valentines. Sweethearts give each other cards. Parents, teachers, and classmates give them, too. Valentines are also a good way to tell friends they're special.

Flowers are popular Valentine's Day gifts. Red roses are favorites. They stand for a loving heart.

Many people give gifts of candy. Children like little heart-shaped candies. Other people give chocolates. Either way, the message is clear. Candy means "You are sweet!"

Candy and flowers are popular Valentine's Day gifts.

At the touch of love,
everyone becomes a poet.
—Plato
(428–348 B.C.)

The greatest thing you'll
  ever learn
Is just to love and be loved
  in return.
—From the song "Nature
  Boy" by Eden Ahbez
  (1908–1995)

CHAPTER NINE

THE POETS' CORNER

Will You Be My Valentine?

Will you be my Valentine?
I know that I am yours.
You are like a tossing sea
And I am like your shores.

You are like an endless wave
And I your waiting sand,
And I will wait forever as
You come and smooth my hand.

I will wait forever, yet
You are a part of me.
I hold you in my arms, while you
Come to me endlessly.

Will you be my Valentine?
I know that I am yours.
I love you with a love that yearns
To be your golden shores.

—Author unknown

An Answer to a Valentine

My true love sent me
   a valentine
All on a winter's day,
And suddenly the cold gray skies
Grew soft and warm as May!

The snowflakes changed
   to apple blooms,
A pink-white fluttering crowd,
And on the swaying
   maple boughs
The robins sang aloud. . . .

O love of mine, my Valentine!
This is no winter day—
For Love rules all the
   calendars,
And Love knows only May!

—Julia Caroline Ripley Dorr
   (1825–1913)

Joining in the Spirit of Valentine's Day

- Make a special Valentine's Day card for a favorite relative. It could be for a brother, sister, parent, grandparent, uncle, or aunt.

- Think of words that rhyme with "love." Then write a Valentine's Day poem. End each line with a rhyming word.

- Is there a home for older people in your community? Visit them on Valentine's Day. Bring cheery cards and flowers. Ask them about their younger days.

- Do you know someone from another country? Ask if his or her country has a special holiday for sweethearts.

Making Queen of Hearts Tarts

Ingredients:

2 ¼ cups all-purpose flour
2 teaspoons baking powder
¼ teaspoon salt
½ cup shortening
1 cup sugar

2 eggs
½ teaspoon vanilla
1 tablespoon milk
2 jars of strawberry or raspberry jam

Directions:

Preheat the oven to 375 degrees Fahrenheit.* Mix the flour, baking powder, and salt in a large bowl. In a separate bowl, stir together the shortening and sugar. Pour this creamy mixture into the first bowl, and add eggs, vanilla, and milk. Mix well. Next, sprinkle a little flour onto a baking board or other flat, clean surface. Pour the mixture on this surface. Use a heart-shaped cookie cutter to cut the dough into about fifty pieces. Place the hearts on a cookie sheet and bake for eight to ten minutes. Cool for about thirty minutes. Once cool, spread jam on each cookie with a plastic knife and top with another cookie. Share the tasty tarts with your special valentine.

Have an adult help you operate the oven.

Making a Valentine Card Scrapbook

What you need:

2 pieces of red or pink
   construction paper
10 pieces of plain white paper
yarn or string
a hole punch

markers, crayons, stickers, and
   glitter for decorating
scissors
glue

Instructions:

1. Decorate both pieces of construction paper with Valentine's Day pictures such as hearts, candy, and cupids. On the piece that will be the front cover, you may want to write "Valentine's Day," the year, and your name.
2. Place the ten sheets of plain white paper in between the two decorated pieces of construction paper. Be sure that the piece you decorated as the front cover is on top. The back cover sheet should be on the bottom with the decorated side facing out.
3. Use the hole punch to punch three holes through the side of the stack of paper. One hole should be near the top, one in the middle, and one near the bottom. Ask an adult for help if it is hard to punch through all of the sheets at once.
4. Cut three 5-inch pieces of yarn or string.
5. Put one 5-inch piece of string through the top set of holes and tie a double knot. If you would like, tie the string in a bow.
6. Repeat Step 5 for the middle hole and the bottom hole.

Now you have a scrapbook ready to hold all of your valentines!

Words to Know

ancient *(AYN-shunt)* very old; often meaning thousands of years old

betime *(bee-TYME)* old word for "early"

knavish *(NA-vish)* tricky

legends *(LEH-jundz)* tales from the past

patron saint *(PAY-truhn SAYNT)* a holy person with special meaning to a group of people

query *(KWEER-ee)* a question

scouts *(SKOWTS)* old word for "mocks" or "rejects"

symbol *(SIM-buhl)* an object that stands for an idea

How to Learn More about Valentine's Day

At the Library

Erlbach, Arlene, and Herbert Erlbach. *Valentine's Day Crafts.* Berkeley
Heights, N.J: Enslow Publishers, 2004.

Landau, Elaine. *Valentine's Day: Candy, Love, and Hearts.* Berkeley
Heights, N.J.: Enslow Publishers, 2002.

Park, Barbara, and Denise Brunkus (illustrator). *Junie B. Jones and the
Mushy Gushy Valentine.* New York: Random House, 1999.

Rylant, Cynthia, and Fumi Kosaka. *If You'll Be My Valentine.* New
York: HarperCollins, 2005.

On the Web

Visit our home page for lots of links about Valentine's Day:

http://www.childsworld.com/links

NOTE TO PARENTS, TEACHERS, AND LIBRARIANS:
We routinely verify our Web links to make sure they're safe,
active sites—so encourage your readers to check them out!

ABOUT THE AUTHOR

Ann Heinrichs lives in Chicago, Illinois. She has written more than two hundred books for children. She loves traveling to faraway places.

ABOUT THE ILLUSTRATOR

Sharon Lane Holm lives in New Fairfield, Connecticut. She just recently illustrated "Twelve Plump Cookies" for The Child's World. Her favorite holiday—is Valentines Day!

Index

A

mwm

A

WWWW